NAWTHIN TO IT DE-AH

...AYUH...

HOW TO TALK YANKEE

BY

GERALD E. LEWIS

ILLUSTRATIONS by

Tim Sample

North Country Press · Unity, Maine

Library of Congress Cataloging-in-Publication Data

Lewis, Gerald E.
  How to talk Yankee / by Gerald E. Lewis ; illustrations by
Tim Sample.
      p.   cm.
  ISBN 0-945980-07-8 (pbk.) : $3.95
    1. English language—Provincialisms—New England—
Dictionaries.   2. English language—New England—Slang—
Dictionaries.   3. New England—Social life and customs—
Dictionaries.   I. Title.
PE2906.L48   1989
427'.974—dc19   88-38431
                                                            CIP

To John Gould, Sage

With thanks to Susan Abel of the Abbott Memorial Library, Dexter, Maine, for her unfailing assistance in this and other enterprises.

INTRODUCTION

In order to talk like a true Yankee, of course, you must be to the manner born. It is unlikely that this guide will enable you to meld unnoticed into the crowd at a Grange dance in New Hampshire, a town meeting in Vermont, or a group of lobstermen on a wharf in Maine; but if there is another one of *you* there, you may fool *him,* and that's almost as good!

Since I am a Mainer, with many generations of ancestry here, my ear is attuned to the speech of this locale, and thus the accents and idioms will most truly fit the State of Maine. However, almost all will be equally suitable throughout Yankeeland.

Supposedly, the Yankee is of few words, his occasional utterances punctuated with many pauses as he whittles, puffs contemplatively on his pipe, or draws circles in the dirt with a stick. "Well naow," he is supposed to drawl, "I ain't so sure about that. . . . " And if a subject is pursued, his opinion may drag on with the pace of a tortoise. However, the case may be quite different, depending on your Yankee.

In the town where I grew up, there was an impoverished family who were notable for their machine gun-like speech. Everybody in that house, and some of their neighbors too, spoke as if they couldn't get the words out fast enough. One time, many years ago, they bought a mattress on credit from a department store in Bath. Having failed to make the payments, they received several threatening letters from the company. Finally, the store sent a truck down, and Brewer was told that unless he made full payment immediately, the company would be obliged to repossess the mattress.

"Goahead," spluttered Brewer. "Takethe goddamthing. Fullofbedbugs anyway!"

So that's how *that* Yankee talked, like a ticker tape machine spewing out the words.

On the other hand, there was Carleton, who spoke in the stock Yankee manner, and with a dreadful nasal twang to boot. He had a date with Sally, a summer girl who had all but given up hope of being asked out. Carleton was no one's Romeo, with his long nose processing any word he uttered; but he did have his own car and Sally was, at last, being asked out by one of the locals.

They were parking near Fort Edgecomb, than which a no more romantic spot could be wished — the dark old fort behind, the Sheepscot River shimmering in the moonlight before them. At length Carleton made so bold as to take Sally's hand. Her heart fluttered.

"Gorry, you've got cold hands," he drawled.

"Oh, what does that mean?" she gurgled, 'cold hands, warm heart' racing through her mind.

"Ba-ad livuh!" (Sp. "liver.")

Then there's the story about the old maid Downeast who'd just received the *Boston Post* cane for being the town's oldest inhabitant. A reporter for the local newspaper came for an interview. To what did she attribute her advanced age?

"Do you smoke?"

"Used to."

"Drink?"

"Been known to."

"Diet?"

"Eat pretty much what I've a mind to."

"Sicknesses?"

"Never."

"Do you mean that in eighty-four years you've never been bedridden?"

"No," she is said to have exclaimed eagerly, "but I had it once in a dory!"

But enough yarns; you'll hear plenty yourself if you keep your ears open. An alphabetical order seems sensible for this little guide, so that's how we'll proceed.

Gerald E. Lewis
Garland, Maine
October 6, 1979

PREFACE TO THE SECOND EDITION

I get a kick out of a story that's told in the western part of the state of Maine.

A group of people, this yarn goes, were waiting on a station platform of the old, narrow gauge Farmington and Rangeley Lakes Railroad. On hearing the train coming around a bend below, they turned toward it, and were horrified to see a man sprinting frantically just a few feet in front of the locomotive.

The onlookers gasped as the participants of the race drew closer, with the man barely able to hold his lead in front of the cowcatcher on the engine. Why didn't the fellow leap to the side, they wondered?

In the bare nick of time, one of the spectators sprang off the platform, grabbed the fleeing man, and snatched him away from destruction as the locomotive thundered by.

"Good heavens!" gasped the rescuer. "Why did you stay in front of that train? Why didn't you jump off the tracks?"

The fellow rescued, it is said, was one of our brethren of Gallic extraction — though he could as well have been "English," as the French call just about everyone else.

"Jump to the side, me? Oh my gosh no! If I lose that good footing, the damn thing catch me for sure!"

An analogy with HOW TO TALK YANKEE wouldn't quite hold up, because this enterprise has been followed not by an engine of destruction, but simply by a freight of success. Still, for the good "footing" they've afforded, I'd like to acknowledge some of the people who've been of much help to me and to this little book.

The manual had its genesis a while back when Miss Darlene Cooley brought me a slim volume entitled, *How to Speak Southern*. It was a clever enough piece of work, "tar arns" as the Secesh rendering of "tire irons" being a good example. I thought that perhaps I could work up a similar thing on New England speech. The Rebs did this Yankee, at least, a favor; and so did Miss Cooley. Thank you, Darlene.

I took my proposal to Phil Treleaven, publisher of Thorndike Press. His reaction was immediate. "Go for it," he said. In addition to this encouragement, as a relative newcomer to the region, Phil was able to spot as Yankeeisms certain phrases that I had accepted as being part of "normal" speech, native that I am. He has been a great help in every way. Thank you, Phil.

That Tim Sample's drawings enliven and illustrate the text goes without saying. Thanks, Tim S.

Paul Garelli, marketing manager at Thorndike, gave the initial and subsequent distributions an enormous boost. I always appreciated his never-failing good humor, and especially the good cheer he brought to the autographing sessions, and he knows what I mean by that. Thank you, Paul.

Tim Loeb, Thorndike's editor, with a sharp mind and a keen ear has been a great help in preparing this second edition. Thank you, Tim L.

I cannot let pass by any opportunity to make public an acknowledgment of indebtedness to my wife, Pat, who is always supportive of anything I try to do right.

Finally, and most important, I must express my gratitude to the readers, to those many who have written to compliment this little book as well as to those who have offered other Yankee terms they think worthy of inclusion. Thanks to all of you: natives, tourists, migrants, and even summer complaints.

Gerald E. Lewis
Garland, Maine
March, 1986

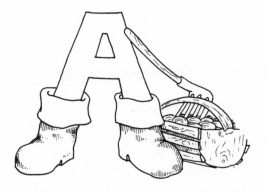

Able. *Adj.*, **physically strong.**

"Dwight heisted that piano up them stairs most all by himself."

"Heard tell. Said he didn't mind the other fellas getting a free ride, but he wished they wouldn't drag their feet."

"He was just kidding them. But he's *able,* Dwight is."

"Ayuh."

Ah.

The letter between "q" and "s."

Aidge-on. *N.*, **(sp. "edge-on"), intoxication.**

Of all slang expressions, those for being drunk constitute one of the longest lists: snookered, slopped, zonked, hammered, stoned, etc., but if you want to talk Yankee, use "aidge-on."

"Ralph had quite an *aidge-on,* didn't he?"

"Ayuh. He drinks like it was coming out of his grandfather's well."

Ain't got nawthin. *Int. phrase,* **this is actually a question which means: "Do you have a drink?" Another form is: "Ain't got nawthin on ye?"**

This is pure Downeast and is essential for anyone learning the language.

Ayuh. *Adv.,* **affirmative, yes.**

A general purpose term which is considered

"Ayuh" is the truest touchstone of genuine Yankee speech. While its pronunciation may vary throughout the region ("eeyuh," "ehyuh"), a Mainer and a Vermonter using it know they're cut out of the same cloth. But let some rusticator from Yonkers try to render it, and the result will be as apparent as a beached whale.

Listen to "The Word" a few hundred times before you try it. The most common mistake outlanders make is to render it with the same inflection, no matter what the circumstances. The Word has infinite shades of meaning. To attempt duplication in cold print would be useless; suffice to say that according to rendition, it can preface an extended observation or abruptly conclude one. It is comforting and it is sarcastic. Listen often to The Word in its sundry applications before you attempt it, and then begin very tentatively, low key — *ayuh.*

B

Bahmy. *Adj.,* balmy.

Use this for irony. Said of fiercely cold temperatures.

"It was cold up there on Spider Lake?"

"Bahmy. Thirty-five below on the last day of February. Never did get much fishing done."

"Well, *wan't* no blackflies to bother *ye.*"

Bail. *V.,* to consume, to impel — often to excess.

"Hot day for fat folks, ain't it?"

"Sure is. Must be ninety in the shade. Man ought to just hole up down *sulla* and *bail* the cider to him."

Or: "By the looks of that front end, them young fellers must have been *bailing* it right to her when they went off the road."

Bake a cake. *N. phrase,* **alternate source of spirits.**

When all Sunday sales of liquor were prohibited, improvident *rumdums* who were dry on the Sabbath were obliged to secure their alcohol in the form of vanilla or lemon extracts. Having imbibed these awful substitutes, they did give off the aroma of a pastry shop.

Sometimes, they resorted to cooking sherry — "Old Salty."

Since the *Green Front* is still closed on Sunday (though liquor may be purchased in restaurants and bars), cakes are still baked on a Sunday, and "Old Salty" swallowed with many a shudder.

Band. *V.,* **to ban, prohibit. Also, "slap a band."**

"I hear if we don't get a rain soon, they're going to *band* the woods." Translation: Open fires will be banned.

Past tense "banded." "They've *banded* fires up above the C.P. Line."

Barge. *N.,* **container.**

One of the many names for the receptacle into which clams are placed as they are dug out of the mudflats: hod, roller, rocker, basket, etc.

Barse-ackwards. *Adv.,* **reversed.**

"Sit yourself the other way in that canoe. You're paddlin' it *barse-ackwards.*"

Baster. *N.,* **(long a), anything of considerable size, see also** *rauncher, honker.* **Also, masculine term of endearment.**

"George got himself an old *baster,* didn't he?"

"*I guess.* That deer dressed out at two thirty-five."

And: "Jim, you old *baster,* where you been all spring?"

Be. *V.*, archaic form of "is."

One of the boys from Barter Island went to the city to sign up for the draft. When asked for his address, he replied, "I come from the Island."

"What Island?"

"Barter Island, for crisakes! What other Island *be thay?*"

Billy-be-damned. *N.*, state of complacency, smugness.

"I got to the mouth of the stream and there was the warden, big as *Billy-be-damned,* and me three trout over."

Bull. *V.*, to work hard.

"We *bulled* right along and got the stone wall laid up in a week's time. I guess it will stand up all right."

Also, *N.*, one who works hard, often without regard to finesse:

"How do you like your new hired hand?"

"Well, he's kind of *gawmy,* but he's an awful *bull.* If he'd take harness, I'd use him to *yahd* pulp."

Bun in the oven. *N. phrase*, state of being pregnant.

By the Old Lord Harry! Exclamation.

"What about the man who bought that boar, Stanley?"

"Well, he was *from away,* moved up here to get out of all that city business, and he bought him a pig. Thing is, he thought he'd bought a barrow, but it *wan't* cut."

"So what happened?"

"Well, when he went to try to cook the thing, it stunk to high heaven."

"No."

"Did. Peeled the shingles right off the shed when they opened the kitchen door. *By the Old Lord Harry,* I got an awful whiff, and I live a mile down the road!"

Can't spin a thread. *V. phrase,* **unable to perform a task.**

"I wanted to sell some cedar down at the mill, but the bar on my chain saw had too much slop in the groove. I paid good money for a new bar, and then the tractor *frigged* up — magneto. So, I got that squared away, and *twitched* out two loads. But now my truck won't start, and the whole outfit just sets there. I *can't spin a thread.*"

Cap'n. *N.,* **Captain. Form of address.**

Along the coast, one who has assumed command of even the most modest of craft is politely referred to as "Cap'n." Sometimes no previous position of authority at all is necessary and a person can be thus greeted merely as a friendly form of address. Similarly, "Cap" or "Cappy" are used, though informally. "Cap'n" itself is the Yankee equivalent of the Kentucky Colonel.

Catch. *V.,* **to freeze, usually temporarily.**

"The pipes caught in our cellar last night. My husband forgot to plug in the heat tapes."

"Well, you can't do *nawthin'* about the weather. And in six months, it'll be hot enough to knock up a goat."

Chahdge. *N.,* **(sp. "charge"), a quantity.**

"You ain't hungry?"

"No, I et an awful *chahdge* for breakfast."

Chimbley. *N.*, **chimney.**
What Santa comes down. Also the glass tube or globe of a kerosene lamp.

Christer. *N.*, **various meanings; a hell raiser, or one who goes** *ramming;* **anything excessive.**
"Wan't that thunderstorm a *christer!"*

Christless. *Adj.*, **along with "christer" and "christly" this is a mildly blasphemous, all-purpose word.**
"I never did think we'd get that *christless* truck out of the ditch. *Wan't* she mired!"

Chum, chummy. *N.*, **form of address, male to male.**
Beware of using these terms. They can be warnings, as are "Mister" or "Mister Man".
"You think so, do you, *Chum!* Why don't we step outside and see if you can back up your yap."
But they can be terms of affection: "Aw cheer up, *chummy;* she's just another girl. . ."

Croose. *V.*, (sp. "cruise"), to inspect forest acreage.
This is normally done, however, by a timber croozer (sp. "cruiser").

Cruncher. *N.*, large deer. See also "rauncher," "baster."
He will probably carry a good set of "horns," not antlers.

Cutting. *N.*, clearing left by logging operation.
If you were *croosing* up in T8-R5, you might see an old *cruncher* in a *cutting*.

Daow. *Adv.*, **negative.**

Downeasters frequently use this expression instead of "No." (*Pronunciation Note:* it rhymes with the name of the late Chairman of the People's Republic of China.)

"Did you get your deer yet?"

"Daow, I can't even see one. I'll give her a try this Saturday, and if it don't go no better, I'm going to hang up my rifle. Out-of-staters getting 'em all anyway."

De-ah. *N.*, (sp. "dear"), **friend,** *chum.*

Don't be alarmed if you hear a couple of rough, tough clam diggers address each other as "De-ah." It's an old custom and indicates not a whit of effeminacy. The greeting crosses all lines of sex and age, and even total strangers may talk to each other thus — provided that they know how to talk Yankee.

Deermeat. *N.*, **flesh of hooved browser.**

Deermeat, not "venison," is the preferred local term.

Desperate. *Adj.*, **hopeless or nearly so.**

"Did you see that woman Ethan had out last night?"

"Some *desperate!* God made her as ugly as he could, then kicked her in the face."

Dingle. *N.*, small storage building or room in a logging camp.

Dite. *N.*, small amount.

Can be same as *scrid*, (q.v.) but can also indicate lateral or vertical measurement.

"Move that jack a *dite* to the left if you want it under the shackle pin."

Drastic. *Adj.*, adventuresome.

"I got to feeling *drastic* and took in the girly show at the carnival."

"How was it?"

"Not worth the money. They said if you really wanted to see something, it would be another five dollars on top of the three I paid to get in! I *wan't* about to go that."

"Don't blame you a mite."

Driver. *N.*, **hard worker.**

"Bertha was the first in town to have her cannin' done."

"*Ayuh,* ain't she a *driver!*"

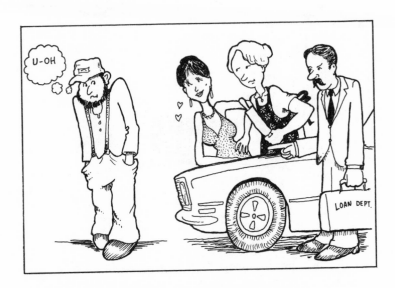

Driving at. *V. phrase,* **attempting, engaged in.**

"What are you *driving at* now, Pete?"

"I'm working two jobs. Have to. I've got a wife, a car payment, and a girl friend; and they're all three thirty days overdue."

Drove up. *V. phrase,* **extremely busy.**

"Eugene is all *drove up* trying to get enough money to buy a new color tv. He dug clams on two tides yesterday."

"Better him than me. I ain't afraid to work, but I ain't afraid not to."

Dub around. *V.,* **to putter without much accomplishment.**

"Pat likes to *dub around* in that canoe, but she still can't paddle a straight line."

Elegant. *Adj.*, **excellent, first rate, has nothing to do with the** *beau monde*.

"How is the chowder?"

"Elegant."

Or: "Why don't we take the day off and go see the Red Sox?"

"Elegant."

Exhilerater. *N.*, **accelerator.**

"Let up on the *exhilerater,* will you, Maggie, while I try to do something with this cussed automatic choke? I wish whoever invented the thing was in hell."

"Ayuh, just something else to *frig* up."

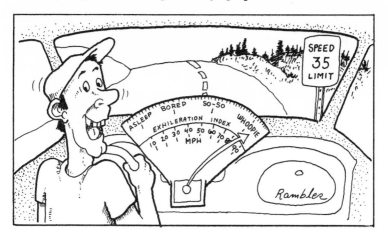

Faht. *N.*, prissy person, meticulous, "nahsty-neat;" applies to both genders. Usually prefaced by "awful old."

"He's an awful old *faht. Never been known* to go anywhere without his necktie on."

Or: "You ain't going to your Aunt Phyllis's for supper?"

"Not if I can help it. She's an awful old *faht;* wants to wash your plate before you've et!"

Faht in a gale of wind. *Characterization,* useless.

"Them plastic grills they put on cars nowadays ain't worth a *faht in a gale of wind.*"

Fallen away. *Adj. phrase,* physically wasted, *gant.*

"Poor Michael has *fallen away* something awful since his wife left him."

"Well, he's moving in with his mother now. She'll fat him up."

Finest kind. *Adj. phrase,* **the best.**

This phrase denoting approbation has, as John Gould notes, been worked to death by tourists and seasonal residents. They use it when they shouldn't (and don't when they should). Probably best to let this one alone until you've heard it often, as its appropriateness is a subtle matter.

Finest kind of pork. *Adj. phrase,* **see above.**

This extension is favored by coastal Mainers. Of obscure origin and having nothing to do with the flesh of the pig, it denotes appreciation of anything from a profitable haul while fishing to a jug of cider to a good looking pan of biscuits.

Foolish. *Adj.,* **dull-witted, mentally retarded.**

"Them *foolish* newcomers left a whole slew of high stumps where they cut on my line. My cow got tangled up in them and ripped her bag, and it cost me twenty-five dollars to have her doctored."

Frig. *V.,* **to dawdle, putter.**

Do not be afraid of using this word in Yankeeland, for it carries none of the salacious connotations associated with it in other parts of the country.

"What you been up to, Si?"

"Nawthin' much. I *frigged* around the garden some this morning and *thrashed* some beans in the afternoon. I've been taking it easy because I've got to put a ring in a bad bull's nose tonight."

The root has a couple other applications:

1. **Frigging.** *Adj.,* **abominable.**

"I can't get this *frigging* halter on right."

2. **Frig.** *V.,* **to botch.**

"That's because you *frigged* up the buckle."

Frog. *V.*, **to labor in a wet area.**
"We *frogged* around in that swamp for three or four hours before we finally found the beaver flowage."

From away. *Prep. phrase*, **transplanted residents.**
"The folks that bought the Pingree place won't let our kids pick raspberries out back of the barn. We've been doing that for years, and besides they admit they're not going to get 'em themselves."
"Well, they're *from away* and don't know no better."
"They'll learn, likely."

Fubdub or Flubdub. *N.*, **one with a compulsive personality, an old** *faht*.
"Jess is such an old *fubdub* — he can't stand to have one tool out of place on his workbench."

Gaffle. *V.*, to snatch or seize.

"Toby *gaffled* onto that barrel of potatoes and *toosted* it right up onto the tailgate, all by himself."

And: "When they offered me a new deal with the interest only eight per cent, I *gaffled* right onto it."

Gannet or gannet-gut. *N.*, a prodigious eater, like the bird from which the term derives.

"Why, I do believe Albion put away four fry pans full of them smelts!"

"Don't doubt it, he's an awful *gannet!* Had four cans of Narragansett to go along with 'em, too. I never see such a *gannet-gut.*"

Gant. *Adj.,* var. of gaunt. Often "ganted" or "ganted out."

"Don't Pete look awful?"

"Ayuh, he's all *ganted* out. That boss of his drives him somethin' fierce."

Garb up. *V. phrase,* to get dressed.

"You'd better *garb up* good and warm. They're calling for fifteen below with winds gusting to twenty-five."

"Colder'n a moose yard."

Gawmy. *Adj.,* clumsy, awkward. Also **gawm,** *n.,* oafish person.

This is an ubiquitous and essential Downeast term. When Winston dropped the fishing trip's supply of beer down the well, his brother called him a *gawmy* bahstud, as he was.

Get done. *V. phrase,* to terminate employment.

"My Pete's going to *get done* at the shoeshop next week. Guess I'll have to go on food stamps, and don't I dread it!"

"Oh, you needn't feel that way, Viney; I had to do the same thing when George got laid off last winter. You'll get used to it. Besides, we've earned them, with all the taxes we pay and all."

Give for. *V. phrase,* to pay.

"What'd you *give for* that new car?"

"More'n I should of. Half of it's plastic, and what's metal you could shoot a BB gun through. I wish they'd put out the old Model A again."

"Who don't?"

Give us. *V. phrase.*

Use this when placing an order at the store. It translates as "Please may I have. . ." or "I would like. . ."

"Give us a pound of them red hot dogs."

Glom. *Adj.* or *V.,* **to grasp.**

"Get your great, *glomming* paws out of that peanut butter fudge. Your sister might want a *dite,* you know."

Or: "When Edwin saw those brand new work gloves going for fifty cents at the auction, he *glommed* right onto the whole lot of them. Nobody else got a single pair."

Go us. *V. phrase,* **to sustain, to "tide over."**

"That hay ought to *go us* through the winter." Also, "go me," "go you," etc.

Or: "I got enough money to *go me* the rest of my life, provided I die tomorrow."

Godfrey mighty! *Oath.*

"Godfrey mighty! I never see anyone so bowlegged!"

"He wouldn't stop a pig in an alley; that's for sure."

Good for. *Adv. phrase,* **capacity, especially vis à vis appetite.**

"How many of these clam fritters are you *good for?*"

Goo-ud. *Adj.,* **normally spelled "good." Often prefaced with "some" or "some old."**

"Mava, this apple pie is *some goo-ud.*"

"Is that so? I made it with McIntosh, too. They ain't supposed to be a pie apple."

"Well, it's *some old goo-ud* anyway."

Gorby. *N.,* **Canada jay. (***Perisoreus canadensis* — **"meat bird," "moose bird," "whiskey jack," "camp thief," etc.)**

This large, soot-colored, ungainly bird is the panhandler of the northern forests. Absolutely fearless, the jay will perch upon the muzzle of a hunter's gun if it thinks it can con the man out of a bite of the sandwich in his pocket.

Old legend held that *gorbies* represent the transmigrated souls of dead woodsmen, thus accounting for their familiarity with man.

Gorry! *Interjection,* all true Yankees use this familiar expression.

"I ice-fished Moosehead opening day, and *gorry, wan't* it cold! Holes skum over fast as you cut 'em."

Grassin'. *Part.* or *Ger.,* pursuit of the fleshly delights *al fresco.*

"Janie, when are you and I goin' *grassin'?*"

"Oh Billy, stop that! You know how my mother won't ever let me out of the house."

Green Front or Dr. Green's. *N.,* state liquor store, so-called because of the color of the exterior in former days.

Also "state store" or "package store."

Greezy. *Adj.,* greasy, slippery.

"The main road is pretty *greezy.* The highway crew should put the sand right to it."

"Well, don't hold your breath. You know what's big and orange and sleeps three, don't you?"

"No, what?"

"State truck."

Gut wadding. *N. phrase,* hay of adequate substance but inadequate nourishment.

"I'm not going to buy any more hay from him. He said it was June cut, but I bet it *wan't* in the barn before August. *Gut wadding* is all it amounts to."

"That won't help your milk check any."

Haythe. *N.*, heath.

Area of soggy, level land. Great place to make the acquaintance of deerflies, as if anyone would want to.

Heavy water. *N. phrase,* **on New England waterways, this has nothing to do with nuclear physics.**

Heavy water is the main current, the place where you want the canoe to go unless you wish to paint some rocks with it along the way.

"Make sure you take the *heavy water* on the left when you pass the big rock that's split in two. It looks deep enough on the right, but it isn't."

Ho-ah, son of a. *N. phrase,* (sp. "whore, son of a"). (Can also be pronounced "hoore," depending on locality. See below.)

As used in New England, this phrase demands explication. Elsewhere in the United States, it may be considered very vulgar, but the farther north you go in Yankee country, the less offensive becomes the epithet. This translation culminates in Aroostook County, Maine — known in that state as "The County" — where the expression has become innocuous and in speech is as common as a conjunction.

In "The County," any male from the age of ten on must say "son of a whore" at least a couple dozen times a day — often many more. If he's a true son, he comes down hard on the "r," since Aroostookers have the distinction, in the New England region where the letter is often ignored, of rolling their "r"'s. He will modify the phrase from time to time with the unblasphemous adjectives "jeezly" or "jeezless" for variety.

"Son of a whore" is an all-purpose phrase in The County. Balky canoes or potato harvesters that keep breaking down are *"sons of whores,"* but so is a canoe that runs straight and a harvester that works without a hitch. A good-sized deer is a *"son of a whore,"* and so is a small one. A close friend is thus termed, as is one's sworn enemy. A predicament is a *"son of a whore,"* but so is good fortune. Paper companies are *"jeezly sons of whores"* as are environmentalists. The B & A railroad, the Governor, your favorite uncle: *"sons of whores"* all. Even women are *"sons of whores!"* No offense intended.

Hold her, Newt. . . *Descriptive phrase.*

Used when something — an automobile, horse, wagon — is about to go out of control.

The entire exclamation is rendered: *"Hold her, Newt;* she's headin' for the meddah"* (meadow; or river, swamp, etc.).

Honk. *V.,* to move, or accelerate.

"He was *honking* it right to her when that deer jumped out in front of his pickup. *Stove* the grill all to hell."

Mother always gave my father credit for coining the phrase, "honk her for home," which is still heard in the region.

"Seven o'clock. I'd better *honk her for home*. We've got company coming."

Honker. *N.*, *baster*, anything large.

Horse. *V.*, to retrieve vigorously.
"You didn't waste much time with that fish."
"No, when I see he was a big one, I *horsed* him right in."

How they actin'? *Interrogative phrase.*
Use this to inquire of a fisherman's luck when you stop by a bridge or culavert (culvert). He'll probably say simply, "Ain't." But if you can, get a look in his creel. And then there's the variant for lobstermen.
"How they crawlin'?"
"Ain't."
He may have caught enough *spiders* that month to pay for his new Chrysler Marine.

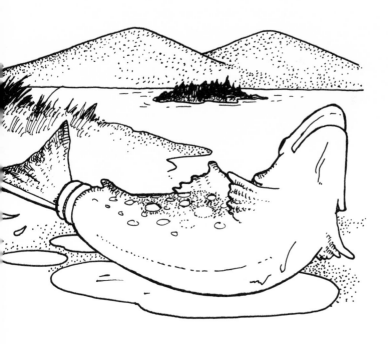

I'll be. *V. phrase*, state of perplexity, bewilderment.

This phrase is used when one is confounded; viz.,

"Well, *I'll be.*"

"What?"

"The *Green Front* is closed. Election Day."

"Well, if we was *desperate,* we could get into that home brew you made last week. But closed, huh? *I'll be.*"

I guess. *Affirmation.* **Contrary to its literal meaning, this translates "without doubt."**

"Your *sport* was mad when he missed a standing shot on that big buck?"

"Mad? *I guess.* He wound his rifle right around a maple tree. Nice new thirty-ought-six!"

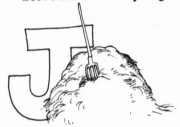

Jo-jeezly. *Adj.* and *Adv.*, ornery or cussed.

"I never see anything so *jo-jeezly* hard to split as that dry oak."

Junk. *N.*, piece of indeterminate size.

You need a good *junk* of salt pork to bake a decent pot of beans.

"Throw another *junk* of wood into that stove."

Also *V.*, to divide into pieces.

Jump down throat. Verbal abuse.

"I guess Elwyn's pigs did get into Fred's garden."

"Ayuh, but Fred didn't have no call to *jump down his throat* like that. Elwyn got 'em out quick's he could, and they didn't do much hurt anyway."

Kahdboo-ud kaht'n. *N.*, test phrase, (sp. "cardboard carton").

When you say this right, you'll be well on your way to acceptable speech. When Yankees travel outside the Northeastern U.S. and meet people who don't know how to talk right, they may be mocked and implored to repeat "Pahk y'r cah in Hahvud Yahd." As far as test phrases go, though, "Hahdah than a ho-ah's haht" may be the best.

Ktaadn. *N.*, Katahdin.

Old spelling (as used in Thoreau's *Maine Woods*) and a good pronunciation for Maine's highest mountain. Used as an index of one's vista.

"My, what a nice view you have here."

"Yes, on a good day you can see clear'n to *Ktaadn*."

Lectricity. *N.*, electricity (sometimes "lectwisity").

When electrical power was introduced into rural homes, innocent folk used to cover unused outlets so the juice wouldn't leak out.

Lift. *V.*, to strike with the fist.

"Clyde was out cold for five minutes."

"*Ayuh*, Frederick really *lifted* him."

Longer than a hard winter. *Adj. phrase*, said of something protracted.

"The preacher goes on and on, don't he."

"Yes, that sermon was *longer than a hard winter*. My roast was burned time we got home."

"We have micro wave."

Lumper's helper. *Characterization.*

Since a lumper does absolutely mindless stevedore work, a *lumper's helper* would hardly be a fountainhead of erudition. In fact, he'd probably be number than a pounded thumb: "wouldn't know enough to pour water out of a boot — with the directions stamped on the heel."

A *lumper's helper* might be *number'n a hake*, but since he does accomplish something in the way of physical labor, he is a cut above a *zero*.

LUMPER   LUMPER'S HELPER

Mackery. *N.*, poison ivy (or "ivory") from "mercury" — *Mercurialis perennis*.

Minge. *N.*, midge.

A little, tiny, teeny-weeny insect with a vicious bite that is disproportionate to its size.

Mister, Mister Man. *N.*, **form of address, male to male. (See "Chum.")**

When called "Mister" by a total stranger in a challenging situation, best be leery. It can be tricky. If you're at the Thistle Inn in Boothbay Harbor, say, and someone says, "Hold up there, *Mister;* what did you say to my *chum* here?" — well, you'd probably settle your bar bill and go someplace else.

More to do than a man on the town. *V. phrase,* **affecting industriousness.**

A person who is *on the town* receives financial aid from same. Someone who has *more to do than a man on the town* might pretend to be busy in order to escape workfare. Or he might be disguising his discomfiture at being unemployed.

Muckle. *V.*, to seize, grasp.

"*Muckle* onto one end of this sofa, will *ye?* I put my back out yesterday and can't lift *nawthin'*."

Mud season. *N.*, fifth season, between winter and spring.

From late November to the middle of March, the provident Yankee carries a snowshovel in the trunk of his car or the back of his pickup. In *mud season,* approximately mid-March, he switches to a spade. Roads and driveways, which had heretofore been dependable, firm gravel surfaces, become axle-deep soup. Town meeting time always comes in *mud season.*

Native beef. *N.*, moose, deer, when harvested out of season. Also known as "some of the Governor's meat."

Nawthin'. *N.*, correct pronunciation of "nothing."

Never been known to. *Adj. phrase*, new occurrence.

Try to become familiar with this common expression and its contrast, *been known to*.

"I don't know what ails that Tony's head. He's *never been known to* get his wood in before Christmas."

Or: "Would you take a drink?"

"Well, *I've been known to*." (Translation: You bet! A drink refused is lost forever.)

Nooning. *N.*, lunch break.

"We took our *nooning* about 11:30."

No-see-um. *N.*, tiny biting insect, *minge.*

When you're off on a fishing trip, or just a walk through a field, and the exposed parts of your body feel dozens of fiery nips, you've made acquaintance with the *no-see-ums* or minges.

Number'n a hake. *Adj. phrase*, stupid.

Why the poor hake — which is delicious corned and served with potatoes and salt pork scraps — is so singled out is unknown to this writer. A *lumper's helper* would certainly be *number'n a hake*.

O. *Pronunciation Note.*

It is impossible to render in print the proper downeast pronunciation of a number of words containing the long "o" sound, such as stone, load, boat, coat, bone. Attempts at phonetical spellings or the use of diacritical marks cannot help here; you'll just have to listen and practice by yourself. You'll be trying to get "stone" somewhere between "stoon" with a short "oo" and "stoo-un." It's hahd.

Old man and old woman. *Adj. phrase.*

Always preface these expressions with the article, as "The old man Brown," or "The old woman Pinkham."

"How'd you find *the old man Scribner* this spring?"

"He wintered out pretty good. Says he's goin' back into sheep if he can find a good Hampshire ram."

"*Ayuh,* they say sheep's the comin' thing now."

On me. *Prep. phrase.* **Use this to attach blame to something or someone other than yourself.**

"I would of had that deer, but my rifle shot to the right *on me.*"

Or: "I lost my pole, tackle box, and a pint with just one drink gone when the canoe tipped over *on me.*"

"How many drinks out of that pint?"

"Well, *thay* was quite a lot left in her."

Pick-ed. *Adj.*, (two syllables), pointed.

"You give that heifer the *pick-ed* end of the stick and she'll move."

Piece out. *V. phrase*, to make do with limited quantity.

"My woodpile is awful low, but I guess we can *piece out* until spring."

Pleg-ged. *Adj.*, (two syllables), var. of "plagued," ornery.

"I had to quit pulling weeds because of them *pleg-ged minges.*"

Pork, had the. *V. phrase*, in bad trouble. Rather curiously, the opposite of "finest kind of pork."

"Yessuh, when that warden found them twelve short lobsters under the life cushions, I knew I'd *had the pork.*"

Pound up. *V.*, physically abuse.

"Jimmy heard what Arthur said about his little sister, and he *pounded* him *up* something fierce."

Prize. *N.*, leverage.

"Put that crowbar under it and give her a good *prize.*"

Quee-uh. *Adj.*, tetched, balmy, not right in the head, queer.

For example, "woods *quee-uh*," is said of someone who has spent too much time in the woods without human companionship.

R. *Pronunciation Note.*

The first rule is to replace the final "r" (or "re") with something close to "ah" or "uh." Thus "there" becomes "thay-uh," "near" becomes "nee-uh," and so forth.

The second rule is to add the final "r" to those given names appearing to lack them — e.g. Lucinder, Amander, Auguster, etc.

The third rule, which is restricted to Aroostook County, is to disregard the first two rules because therre, the morre "r"'s the betterr.

Ramming. *V.*, on the town.

"Al's not coming to work today?"

"No, called in sick. He was *ramming* around all last night and won't be worth *nawthin'* this morning."

Red flannel hash. *N. phrase*, delicious remnants of boiled dinner with beets.

Should be ground quite fine, served with vinegar.

Reef. *N.*, **strong tug.**

"If you'll stop *frigging* around and take a good *reef* on that line, we can haul this old scow off the rocks before sunset."

Reverse nod. *Non-verbal language.*

If you want to be accepted as a native, don't wave; give the reverse nod. Properly delivered, the Yankee greeting has the chin lifted, the mouth open as if inhaling a gulp of air. This is perfectly acceptable and usual when drivers of two vehicles pass each other, or when a driver acknowledges a pedestrian. Another acknowledgment while driving consists of the index finger lifted slightly from the steering wheel. Never a wave of the hand, just the one finger.

Rig. *N.*, **unusual device, outfit, or person.**

Jerry-built contrivance: "What kind of a *rig* is that you got for a fan belt on your tractor?"

"Well, the regular one busted and I made up one out of a piece of harness. Guess I can piece along with it till I get a new one."

Or: Bizarre attire: "You can't imagine what *rigs* they wear down in the city. I see one feller with a long black cloak, gum rubbers, a coonskin hat — and ear rings!"

Or: Outlandish person: "That Peter is an awful *rig*. He's taking out them two Williams sisters, and I hear they both got a *bun in the oven*."

Right around. *Adv. phrase*, **early, betimes.**

"You're *right around* this morning."

"Man has to get up before breakfast if he wants to make a dollar nowadays."

Rumdum. *N.*, **a sot.**

Rumdums used to have to *bake a cake*.

Scrid. *N.*, tiny portion, see also "dite."

"Want a little more of this roobub pie?"

"Well, I might take just a *scrid*, thank you."

SCRID OF ROOBUB PIE

Scurvy. *Adj.*, dirty or villainous.

"Did you see the crew that got off that trawler?"

"Gorry, wasn't they a *scurvy*-looking outfit! Hadn't washed for a month, I'll bet."

"I know it. Enough to gag a maggot."

Shedder. *N.*, lobster in stage of moult.

Usually, this "soft shell" brings a lower price.

Skinboat. *N.*, windjammer cruise craft.

The etymology derives from either the amount of overt epidermis on deck or the covert activities below.

Slack salted pollack. *N. phrase*, regional delicacy.

Coastal dish, Sunday supper in days of yore, it is pollack which has been split, salted, and dried in the sun. Served with potatoes and salt pork gravy. Sad to say, nowadays the closest source is Campobello Island, Canada.

Slicker'n a smelt. *Adv.*, easily.

"We kept to the right hand side in the rips below Russell's Point, found the *heavy water,* and put that 20-foot Guide's Model through there *slicker'n a smelt.*"

Slimpsy. *Adj.*, sleazy, of poor quality, cheap.

"She was braggin' up that bargain coat she got at the lawn sale, but *wan't* that *slimpsy* goods?"

"*Ayuh.* Think I saw that coat in Martha's sale last year."

Some. *Adv.*, very. Often "some old."

Peculiarly, this word, which is usually adjectival, serves as an adverb in Yankeeland: "some old homely," "some pretty."

"Joe was *some ugly* when he found out he had to register his twelve foot canoe if he wanted to put his little electric outboard on it."

"I don't wonder. Way it is now, if you had a pair of waterwings and an egg beater, the State would say you was a motorized craft and stick a number on you."

Spaded. *V.* or *Adj.*, spayed.

"I had to get my Judy *spaded* before she got knocked up by that Pekinese next door."

"That thing! If I had that critter, I'd stick a handle in him and use him for a mop!"

Spider. *N.*, lobster on the coast, a frying pan inland.

The latter kind of *spider* must be of cast iron, seasoned by servicing crockfuls of salt pork, hundreds of trout, and a dozen hind quarters of deer. It should be wiped clean, never washed in detergent.

Spleeny. *Adj.*, sissified.

"The Beck boy is awfully *spleeny*."

"Well, the apple doesn't fall far from the tree. Look where he comes from. I've seen his father take a bite of potato chip, and then throw away the part he'd held onto; dirty, don't you know. It runs in the family: they're all soft."

Sport. *N.*, hunting or fishing client.

"You know, a guide's got to have a lot of patience. I had a *sport* last week who was so *numb* he was trying to throw out flies with a bait casting rod."

"That ain't nothing. I had one trolling with a surf casting outfit that would land a whale."

"We're lucky they're not all that bad."

State of your mind and stem of your constitution. *Interrogatory phrase,* part of a male-to-male inquiry concerning health and general condition.

"How's the *state of your mind and the stem of your constitution?*"

Answer: "Straight up," or "hanging straight down," depending.

Stave. *V.*, to move vigorously, often irresponsibly; to break, esp. to break-in or up.

"Henry was here for about two hours, full as a tick and *staving* around, looking for a fight. Finally his old lady showed up, took him right by the ear and fetched him home. Didn't he let the blats out of him."

Or: "Get ahold of that ram b'fore he *staves* up the whole barn."

Or: (*past tense*) "Too bad about your car gettin' *stove* up by that tree, Anne. How fast was it goin'?"

Stemmy. *Adj.*, concupiscent.

"They say that eating oysters makes you *some stemmy.*"

"That's what my uncle Albert thought. He said he had six of them for supper on his wedding night, but only five of them worked."

Straight ahead. *Affirmation,* assent.

"What do you say we call in on those two school teachers from Atlanta who are renting the Harvey camp this summer?"

"*Straight ahead.* They looked pretty good."

Stramming around. *V.*, what young children are doing after they've been told to "Set still!"

Street, over street, down street. *Adj. phrase,* in town.
"Where's Kathy?"
"She went *over street* to get some medicine, but she should be back in two shakes of a lamb's tail."

Sulla. *N.*, cellar or basement.
Usually preceded by "down." Holman Day wrote a fine verse about an old feller who breaks his wife's pet jug — and nearly his own neck — when he goes *down sulla* to fetch his nightly cider. She is very concerned — about the jug.

Supper. *N.*, end-of-the-day-meal.
Get this straight. You eat breakfast in the morning, dinner at noon, and supper in the evening. Lunch is something you carry along with you in your dinner bucket.

Take a fit. *V. phrase,* **to yield to impulse.**

"I *took a fit* to buy me a beagle pup. They're supposed to be good with kids."

"Is he?"

"Oh yes, wouldn't bite a biscuit."

Thay. Alternate pronunciation of there.

"I hear where *thay's* going to be a new preacher over to the Methodist Church."

"*Ayuh.* Young feller. Plays guitar during the hymn-singing."

"He won't last long."

"Nope."

Thrash. *V.,* **thresh.**

Tomatoes. *Pronunciation note.*

This is to be pronounced with a long "a," of course. Anyone who'd say "tomahtoes" would put them into a clam chowder.

Took. *V.,* **struck.**

"The bullet *took* that coyote just behind the shoulder, and he still run five hundred yards, I'll bet. Can you imagine it?"

"They're tough, that's for sure. Good thing you done him in though; they're no earthly good."

Toost. *V.,* **to lift.**

"We cut a long maple pole, got a good *prize,* and *toosted* the truck right out of that ditch."

Town fathers. *N. phrase,* **town selectmen.**

Prob. obs. with fem. lib.

Tunk. *N.* or *V.,* **a light blow.**

"I got to get me a new shotgun. Mine won't throw out the shell without I *tunk* it every time. Missed a good chance on a rabbit that way yesterday."

Or: "You've got to *tunk* that nut to get it started."

"Tunk it! What I'd like to do is *whale* it with a top maul. I've been trying to get this magneto off for an hour."

Turned around. *Adj.,* **lost.**

A euphemism. A hunter may have spent the better part of an afternoon getting out of a cedar swamp on a cloudy day when he'd forgotten his compass, but if asked why he's late for supper will note merely that he'd been "turned around." If he spent the whole day in there, he'd been "turned around some." If he had to spend the night in that swamp, he'd been "some turned around."

Rural folk get "lost" in the city, but "turned around" in the woods.

Twitch. *V.,* **to pull a log, or logs, with horse or tractor.**

Ugly. *Adj.*, ill-tempered.

"The *old man* Brown was *some ugly* about them kids swiping his apples."

"Well, it *wan't* the apples they took. It was they clumb up in the tree and shook it and then just picked up a few before they skedaddled. Left all the rest bruised on the ground."

"I don't blame him then. I'd be *ugly* myself."

Unthaw. *V.,* to thaw (!).

Used up. *Adj. phrase,* exhausted; worn out.

"Them carnival fellas looked pretty *used up* after the Wagstaff boys got through with them."

"*Ayuh.* I guess they took quite a *thrashing.* Maybe that'll learn 'em not to cheat."

Or: "How'd you find your Uncle Harold?"

"Well, he says he's all *used up,* but I see where he's got in his next winter's wood already."

"Sounds about right. Harold always was tougher'n a bagful of hammers, for all his complaining. How old is he now?"

"Just turned eighty-three. He'll see another round one, though."

Vah or Vy. An expression of mild rebuke or tease used in coastal Maine.

"*Vah,* you're asking Stephen over for supper? I thought you didn't like him."

Very-close veins. *N. phrase,* varicose — more common than you might think, esp. among older folk.

Walk it to. . . *V. phrase*, this denotes various types of concentrated effort.

"I see where Fred's put up his new page wire fence around that pasture. Said he did it in just two days."

"Yup. He must have *walked it* right *to* her."

Or: *"Walk it to* him." This is a common shouted encouragement at a pugilistic encounter, whether the participants are gloved or not.

Or: "That new-seeded piece is coming right along. You ought to get a decent second cutting."

"Ayuh, I *walked* the dressing *right to* it."

Wan't. *V.*, wasn't.

"Wan't them lovely fireworks over to the Fair?"

"Elegant, I liked the part where they acted out the hen laying the egg, all in the fireworks."

"Eeyuh, that was somethin'."

Or: "That *wan't* much of a supper over at the Firemen's."

"I guess. They said it was going to be baked beans, and maybe it was if you call something out of a can a baked bean."

"Ayuh, and store-boughten rolls and pie. . ."

"They said they wanted to give us Auxiliary a night off. Well, I say we better go back on."

Wany. *Adj.*, said of boards with bark still attached.

Were. *V.*, to talk like a native, you may use this as a singular verb.

"I *weren't* going to the Harmony Fair this year, but the old man drove me." (forced me)

Whale. *V.,* **to strike vigorously.**

"How'd you run your fence so tight?"

"Well, I made me a new maul out of a piece of rock maple, got a box to stand on, then I *whaled* the bejeezus out of the posts. Man can't run a good fence unless he's drove those posts right down hard."

"Look awful pretty."

"Nothing prettier than a tight fence."

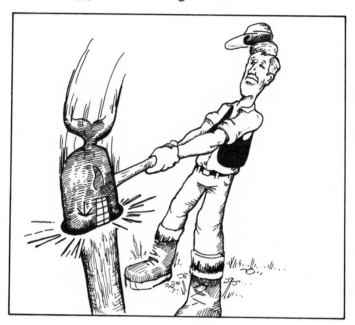

What is or what are. *Interrogatory,* **a curious circumlocution indicating that the questioner wishes to pursue a subject.**

"*What is,* Eben going to buy a new manure spreader?"

"*Daow.* He won't buy it. Says he just wants to try her out. He will, till he cleans out his barn."

Or: "*What are they,* going to plow the Henderson Road now them new folks have built in there?"

Where would a man find. . . Employ this as an oblique opening bid in a dicker.

"Where would a man find a good shoat? Mary says that with the price of pork what it is, we ought to keep a pig."

"Well, I got a couple good ones, but I figured to hold onto 'em. They do better feedin' against each other, don't you know. I might let one go, though, if the price was right."

And so on.

Wicked. *Adv.*, very.

"How was the horsepulling?"

"Wicked good. Seth took top money with his new team."

Wind. *V.*, (Long "i"). See "bail."

"How come you went and bought a new chain saw?"

"Well, I was *junking* up that old sugar maple that got blowed down last weekend. And I was *winding* it right to her when I struck an old spile half a foot inside the bark. 'There,' says I, 'good excuse to buy me a new saw,' which I should of done two years ago. She's a corker, my new one — takes out a real good chip."

Xtry. *Adj.* or *N.*, something in addition. (Got to get an "x" in here.)

"I *wan't* going to trade, but when the dealer said he'd give me something *xtry* on my old Chevy, I took him up on it. Now I wish I had her back."

Yahd. *V.*, to haul.

About the same as *twitch,* except that usually a quantity of logs are *yahded.*

Also, *N.,* a place in the forest where deer dwell in the winter: a "de-ah yahd."

Yahn. *V.*, yarn. To haul or drag — usually connotes futility.

"I had to *yahn* that trailer all around the camping area three times before Mother found a place she'd let me park it."

Ye. *Pronoun,* pronounced "yee" or "yeh", 2nd person, sing. or pl.

This old-fashioned word survives as a localism.

"How be *ye*" is a common greeting, especially among older folk.

Yo! *Interj.,* hail.

Used when trying to locate someone who is at a distance — down in the far pasture, maybe, or lost in the woods — because of the sound's carrying qualities.

"Yo-o-o!"

Shorter form employed to stop a passing vehicle when you recognize an occupant and remember you wished to speak to him.

"Yo!"

Yow-uns. *N.*, young ones.

"My granddaughter Lisa asked her mother to buy her some overalls for her first day of school."

"*Ayuh,* thay's no accounting for what *yow-uns* want to wear nowadays."

Zero. *N.*, cipher, a person of no importance, nonentity.

"That Jason is an absolute *zero.*"

"Ain't he, though. Don't know enough to sit down when he's tired."

THE END